Allow Your Soul To Lead

Volume 3

The Love of The Soul
&
The Process of Deliberate Alignment

A Channeled Text
Healing Series

Cindy Edison

Table Of Contents:

WELCOME

Greetings Dear One,

As we embark on our third volume of the series Allow Your Soul To Lead, we'd like to thank you for your participation so far. If you have not read volumes one and two, it is a good idea however it is not necessary for the advanced student. If you have trouble in understanding, know the understanding will come as your awareness expands to include it. Each has his or her understanding level and it is individual, none better than the next. Whatever your interest, we welcome you to this third volume entitled, The Love of the Soul.

In this volume, we will explore the expansive nature of the Soul and how the aspects play a role from the higher perspective of the Soul. Your Soul, individual and all-inclusive simultaneously, is the eternal piece of you that is referred to as God.

In this volume, we will offer a perspective of the current dominating collective understanding of the word God from many angles, many religious understandings and how the current collective vibration of this understanding relates to the Soul of you and how this perspective offers the light so many are seeking. Most teachings today however, are still being taught from a lower vibration that teaches that God is outside of the 'self', or the Soul of the individual. It is an un-evolved teaching that is stuck in linear time by those who are teaching it. This is why the result of this teaching is rampant confusion, struggle, discord and pain. Within this naturally evolving Universe, this energy, this vibration rather, is fear based and it has and continues to slow the expansion of the collective human consciousness. It is pushing against its own natural state of being. Opposition is the contrasting factor, manifested through fear based thinking. This is the reason there is corruption upon your planet; corruption in the form of bullying in a sense where power comes in. However, the power you hold within you is the power of, what is referred to by some, as God.

Many will say we are blasphemic beings because of our teaching that you, your Soul and God, are One in the same, however no statement has been more true. To believe anything less of yourself and Who You Really Are is a fear-based belief, for in God, in You, there is only Love. This is the Truth that will set you free.

It is from the fear of the current teaching of the word 'God' that the word blasphemy falls you see. It is in the fear of your own power that you may refuse to look in other directions for a higher understanding. It is in the teachings of those before you that you have bought and paid the price for their beliefs. It is up to you to seek higher understanding of who you truly are which is the purpose of this healing series. It is a series of teachings that heal through the understanding of our words for there is deep healing in truth, you see. There is no fear here. Only love.

As we move through these next pages, we encourage you to open your mind and as you are understanding our words, examine your beliefs around your own thoughts about what you are feeling as you read. Your beliefs, not those that were handed to you or in some cases, beat into you, for those beatings whether through words or by hand, were acts and manifestations of fear in another. It is time to release all fear of who you are and explore the power that is within you and the power you possess to heal yourself from the fear of others. It is in fear that you suffer. It is in love that you thrive.

We welcome you once again upon this journey of hope, peace and love in the discovery of who you truly are.

We are grateful you are here.

We are Josef.

PRELUDE TO THE WORK

As we begin this third volume, we move forward with the knowing of certain things explained in Volumes 1 and 2, the most important for this Volume being the Soul is your Godness. Your Soul is the piece of God that makes you individual. Your Soul is where your power is and within your Soul, the make up of your Soul as it were, is the pure vibration of what is called God.

Many have been taught and therefore believe that "God" is an entity unto himself who sits about and judges. In their minds, he has the power to 'do away with you' or to grant you many wishes based on the good behavior you live, sometimes out in public and sometimes behind closed doors but always within the mind. This god some speak of allows children to die, takes loved ones away and allows world famine and destruction because of hidden reasons only he is privy to. This god shows his wrath for thoughts and things he does not approve of and wipes out entire countries with the flip of a natural disaster switch. This god imposes heartache and suffering as he sees fit and you are not to question this god for he has his reasons.

Our beloved partner, Cindy, has just replaced her natural "G" with "g" when referring to this illusory character as not to imply respect. We do not wish to confuse so we agree with her movement on this. But we digress.

This god we have vaguely described probably seems familiar in one regard or another based on the teachings you may have received or may have even taught yourself. Regardless of the way in which this information has come to you, we are moving forward with our perspective, the perspective of your Soul, the God within you, and we encourage you to open your heart to receive these words. Of course, it is your choice whether you choose to move forward with this teaching or not however we ask you to consider, for a short period of time, this alternate perspective with which to uphold your belief in a higher power and how that higher power operates. We ask you to consider the science of your planet and the experiences with which you consider choosing your own beliefs. We ask that you consider and take into account what you have witnessed and experienced for yourself and how these words make you feel, outside of the self-imposed fear you may have in reading them.

Our partner remembers a time when she too believed some of what we have portrayed here as god. When we began offering opportunities for different kinds of thoughts and theories, she initially shied away, believing she may be 'punished' for thinking outside of the Bible's box of definitions of who this god is. After all, it had been years of teaching, years of input that was now being challenged. But one day, in one moment, her questions about what she was hearing took precedence and she began seeking in a different direction. She recalls it this way...

"I had been watching a preacher on television I had seen many, many times and I respected the way he taught what was written in the Bible. At that time, I had read it through two, maybe three times in its entirety and believed I had a good understanding of what was being taught. I don't remember what he said in that moment but something was different. As it turns out, it was me. In that moment of question, I turned off the TV, closed my Bible, looked up and said, "I don't believe you are contained in this book anymore. I'm asking you now to teach me yourself."

That day her life changed and new opportunities began to present themselves; opportunities for learning a new way of life, a way that focused more on love than fear and what she ultimately discovered for herself, as you will if you allow it, was when you seek love, you find it in many places, mainly within yourself. It is not outside of you nor does it depend on the approval of anyone or anything in order to be experienced.

The love that all seek is found within the Soul of you. This God vibration of pure, positive energy that creates universes is the breath of you. When you pray to your god, you are praying to your Soul that is within. Jesus said, "the kingdom of God is within you." He was referring to your Soul. Your Soul is the Kingdom. It is where your power is and it offers all understanding for you, at your request.

In this Volume 3, we will explore the love of the Soul and how, when your Soul leads you - vibrationally through Love - your life is the experience you, as your Soul, chose before you arrived in this plane of existence. As we've said, you have had many experiences on earth as the human aspect of your Soul. You've had many experiences in other realms as well, as other aspects of your Soul and you will continue to experience eternal life, at all stages and in all states of consciousness as your Soul evolves.

Your Soul that is the pure vibration of God is in constant motion forward. It seeks only to expand itself as the love of God that is its makeup. Through this expansion, It chooses Its experiences that match the momentum that will manifest the experiences that result in that desired expansion. This is the process of life, the eternal life of the Soul.

The experience you are having now on earth was chosen as all are chosen. The timing of this choice was based on the imminent vibration of the collective consciousness of the planet and the forethought that brought you here today.

The consciousness that is available now has never been before. Our partner is asking "isn't all consciousness the evolved consciousness of what was before?" And we say absolutely it is. However, in this case, the case of the current consciousness, it is at a place of sheer movement. By this we mean there has never been opportunity before for this type of shift; it is the shift of the universe. It is the shift that involves not only humanity as the collective driving force on the planet, but the collective consciousness of the earth as well. Mother Gaia, as she is commonly referred to, has shifted into this consciousness too and as she continues to expand to the fifth dimension of existence and beyond, she has, along with the universe, opened the doors (so to speak) for all of humanity to shift with her as well. This means she has risen above the collective fear-based vibration and as she continues to rid herself of the denseness that has plagued her and all who inhabit her, the choice of all who inhabit her is put before them, meaning the human race. The animal kingdom and the vegetation have already gone with her, you see as they inherently live each day as their Soul. Humans, however, housing active free will and holding old paradigm belief systems, not so much. The human-race, the human collective consciousness is and has been riddled in fear for eons. Because of the expansion of the earth's consciousness, this movement has offered a new timeline of sorts. It is a timeline of love that offers a vibration that lies above that of fear. It is the vibration of the New Earth and is available through the expanding of your own consciousness, your own vibration. It is lived through your thoughts, your beliefs and the vibration that you manifest each day.

You create from the inside out. You live what you believe and the vibration that is on the inside of you is manifest on the outside. When we say your alignment is everything, we mean the alignment with the consciousness of the Soul as opposed to the alignment with that of your ego.

Through this volume, we will offer examples and exercises that will assist in expanding your vibration. This will allow the momentum to build in the direction of love.

We are not here to challenge your beliefs or the beliefs that have been handed down to humans through centuries of living on planet earth. We are here, however, to offer a new perspective. It is the perspective of the evolved consciousness that is now available, as the perspective you currently hold is one that was available thousands of years ago. It served its purpose for the consciousness that created it. Now, there is a new plane of existence that is the manifested evolved consciousness of the old. It is time for change.

Welcome aboard.

FEELING THE LOVE OF THE SOUL

Our partner, throughout our relationship, has, many times, said to us, "Ok, I understand what you're saying but show me how; what does it feel like?" in relationship to something we were teaching her. We understand this concept of the human when the human is in doubt of his/her own ability to understand their true self. It is the experience that teaches. Our friends Abraham have taught, "words don't teach" for many years. The power of the experience of You, meaning the power to feel who you truly are, is held within you. The Soul 'feels' while the ego 'thinks'. It is all available through your awareness of it and as your awareness expands to include whatever you desire, you welcome it into your vibrational awareness - by choice - and this choice is one of a new perspective.

The love of the Soul, the feeling of that we mean to say, is something that is felt through your active vibration. Sometimes, we hear our human friends say, "his eyes were dead" meaning there was no life to 'see' from the outside in. This is a vibrational seeing of course. It is the nonrecognition of what you are and what you are seeing in another in the human plane of existence. Our partner is starting to make a face at this line of reasoning so we will take a different route.

Feeling the love of the Soul, simply put, is the feeling some of you have experienced, of being 'in love.' Now, this feeling is sometimes mistaken however it is a reflection of your vibrational awareness. Many are judged by others and we hear them say, "they don't know what love is" or "that is not love" and in many cases, technically speaking, they are correct however the judgment is misplaced.

All 'feelings' or acknowledgments of love are recognized vibrationally. This means what one feels and calls love may not be equivalent (in human terms) to another's feeling or recognition of love. Love cannot be taught. It is felt vibrationally.

You see, you cannot experience what is not in your awareness and this goes for the feeling of love as well. All love is felt by the level of awareness that is available and all is as intensely felt to the holder of that awareness. We will attempt to simplify this statement.

The term "love" has many different definitions by human standards and is used in many ways. In our description, and how it relates to the subject of Us and your Soul, Love is a vibration. It, like all vibrations, has a specific tone and physical 'feeling' that it manifests as all vibrations do. The Love vibration is the pure vibration that contains no denseness. It has no element of fear nor does it manifest fear-based physical responses.

We say this as we have watched many of you 'kill' in the name of love by way of religious beliefs or maim in the name of love as if love carries an element of revenge of some kind. This is never the case. Love cannot, by utter definition, carry fear or revenge in any sense; or the imposing of any kind of control over another has nothing to do with love, but everything to do with fear.

The misconception about love is widespread and in order to be in alignment with your Soul and to ascend to the New Earth vibrational dimension, alignment is necessary for in alignment, there is not denseness. The way is made clear through your vibrational asking.

Those of you who have been 'in love' or have loved in any sense whether it be a pet or a spouse, boyfriend or girlfriend, or your child perhaps, are sometimes under the misconception that the love is made possible because of this counterpart in your equation. This is not the case either. This is a misconception that has brought many to their knees so to speak.

Love is never 'found' outside of the Self. The love you are offering or perhaps believe you are receiving from another is the love of your Soul, manifest. It is the vibrational manifestation of the vibrational connection to the Soul of you which is recognizing the Soul - the matching vibration of the Soul, the Oneness as it were - in another.

You see because the Oneness of the Universe is comprised of the Souls of All, when that vibration is recognized in another, the recognition is that of the connection to Source. It is the finding of another puzzle piece of yourself you see. In essence, you have recognized yourself in the other.

When you feel love for anything and are assuming, based on what you were taught perhaps, that it is because of anything or anyone outside of yourself, you are, in fact, feeling Self Love. You are feeling the Love of the Soul.

Our friends Abraham teach "get happy" to gain alignment. This is some of what they are teaching. When you are feeling love of any kind, you are in alignment with your Soul and it is impossible to be in alignment and not 'be happy'; and not be peaceful; and not be joyful from the inside. This is never caused by anyone around you but perhaps encouraged and expanded. This feeling is available to all who seek it from the Source of Its Being. Never from outside 'sources."

The love offered by the Soul is the indication of your alignment with your purpose, you see. Many are confused as to what their 'purpose' is and what they are 'supposed to do'. This is due to their non-recognition of their connection to their own Soul's knowing, for your Soul, the Soul of the All, has no questions. The Soul knows the purpose and that under-lying purpose is always the expansion of love. Each time you 'feel' the vibration of that Oneness, the in-love feeling you attribute to others, you are expanding your vibration and offering more pure love vibration to the Universe.

All vibration is emitted. It is sent out so to speak and is answered immediately - in the blink of an eye even - by the Universal law of attraction. This Universal law, like all other Universal laws, never fails. It is an ongoing, moment by moment asking and answering of vibration. When vibrations match up, manifestation happens. So then, it stands to reason that if you are emitting or sending out the vibration of pure love, you will experience the manifestation of that love as it is matched by the Universe. This 'matching' manifests as opportunities for more of the same. It is at this point vibrational agreement happens and the feeling or the experience of that vibration manifests.

Abraham teaches Ask and It Is Given in this sense as well. The Asking is vibrational and the Giving is the matching of that vibration and is Given by way of the Universal law. You've seen stickers, bumper stickers or electronic postings that say, "be mindful of the vibration (or energy) you are bringing into this space." This is the reason for the 'caution' when carrying your vibration around with you. It is as a scent, if you will, that follows and precedes you simultaneously, and is 'picked up' so to speak by all who come in contact with it. It 'spreads itself out' and attracts the matching vibration surrounding it.

Think of it as a big magnet and wherever you go, you are attracting the counterpart. When the agreement happens, the 'slamming together' happens and the connection is made. Hence, manifestation.

So, if you are emitting fear-based vibrations as opposed to the vibration of love, all those fear-based vibrations that surround you as you walk through your life, are being called so to speak. They are calling or signaling each other. The same goes for the vibration of love, however the manifestations are very different, opposite in fact, and the feelings you feel from each are your indication of where your vibration is in relation to your alignment with your Soul. If you are living in chaos, you are vibrating fear. If you are living in peace, you are vibrating love. Abraham teaches, "clean up your vibration." Better advice has never been given.

Living the love of the Soul is really New Earth living. It is a vibrational state of being that attracts love on a continual basis. It is the perspective of the Soul in all cases. Each time you choose love over fear, you are choosing expansion of not only your human aspect but of your Soul and the Universe as well. This is the momentum that will shift the collective consciousness from fear to love, one Soul at a time.

HOW THE SOUL LOVES

This is an interesting topic, this love topic of the Soul, for the Soul IS love you see. So, this would be as if we said to you, describe how your eyes see. The response to this, of course, is the eyes transmit a vibration and it is translated into what you see. The Soul loves in the same manner. Loving is the Soul's purpose and you are Its manifestation in the third dimensional realm.

The Soul is made up of pure positive love vibration therefore it cannot help BUT love. This is why and how the 'new human' exists in the fifth dimensional New Earth. By vibration. All relationships on the New Earth, if we were speaking of a physical place that is, are vibrationally held.

The vibration of Love contains all things that exist in the pure vibration meaning the awareness, the expansive awareness of this vibration is where it all happens, so to speak. The vibration of love carries with it all possibilities. This means that this is the 'place' vibrationally speaking, that holds all desires held by you, the human aspect - individually and collectively.

As you journey through your physical life, you 'store' (for lack of a better term at this juncture) all your desires that are held in love and are without the fear vibration, in 'escrow'. In other words, and in the words of our dear friends Abraham, in the Vortex. This is where the possibilities are you see and they are realized through your expanded awareness and vibrational agreement of and to them. That is how they manifest and express themselves as your physical reality.

This expanded vibrational agreement is otherwise known as your awareness. Our partner is visualizing this as a band of some sort. It has a width to it and as you grow spiritually, this growth is 'measured' by your awareness. It is in this awareness that possibilities exist. The possibilities we speak of are vibrational.

Vibrational possibilities turn into probabilities as the denseness falls away. As you expand your consciousness by way of choosing love over fear, you are in essence, cleaning up your vibration. Our partner tends to think of this process as dusting; getting rid of the 'dirt' so to speak.

Each time you choose love over fear, you expand your consciousness, your vibration. The feeling of love is a manifestation of the Soul's vibration and the closer you get to it, meaning each time you choose alignment with your Soul, you are in a loving state where all possibilities exist.

The Soul doesn't 'try' to love, it just does. It cannot help but love for through love, the Soul expresses itself. It is the love of God and is the essence of who you really are. This is what the saying, "With God all things are possible" describes. This truly means when you hold the pure vibration of God, of your Soul, all things are possible. In other words, when you are in alignment with your Soul, all knowing is available to you.

Picture this if you will... your Soul is the God within you. This 'God' knows all the possibilities that exist because of the awareness that It is. This awareness, the pure vibration of this God you refer to, is the purest vibration that holds no ego senses. Without the ego senses - or as our partner refers to them, the ego's signage - there is nothing holding it back from knowing. The Soul is never held back from knowing anything for it knows all that is available in each moment. That is not to say the All of the moment doesn't shift in each moment! It does. Each time a human aspect chooses then experiences love over fear, it results in expansion of this pure vibration. As the Vibrations change - in this case, as the vibrations expand, the possibilities expand as well. There is nothing that is not contained in this momentary vibrational stance for it is the true essence of All that is.

So, when you are sitting in this pure vibration meaning when you are in alignment with your Soul, you are feeling this loving vibration as well. This is where the Soul leads from. It is where your knowing lies. It is where the Soul of you expresses Itself as Love. When you are feeling authentic love, you are expressing the Soul in the physical realm and you are experiencing Oneness with what you may refer to as God.

When you are feeling love for someone, what you are experiencing is the human aspect that is you, in alignment with the Soul of you who is naturally in alignment with the Soul of the perceived other and simultaneously with their human aspect as well. This is true Oneness. It is the recognized feeling of love by way of the unified Soul. It is the Love that this Soul of you, or God if you prefer, exists as. It is the Love of the Universe at its best.

This Soul recognition you experience and refer to as 'being in love', is the recognition (on the Soul level) of the Oneness of the Universe. It is the ultimate definition of co-existing. As you begin to recognize this more in yourself, simultaneously, you will molt into recognizing it in others and soon you will begin to recognize it in all things for all things hold potential. All things experience the physical existence, the physical life, as vibrational beings. It matters not the size nor the perceived purpose by humanity. The umbrella picture shows the equality of all things, all participating and all as important as the One within it.

This pure vibration, this universal-sized consciousness puzzle if you will, contains all pieces and without one, the Universe is not complete which cannot happen for the Universe is the example of balance and vibrational control for there are no coincidences and nothing ever happens at the wrong time, universally speaking, from the Soul's perspective. When this perspective is received and understood, and ultimately lived by the human collective, there will be peace on earth and as a result and by simultaneous movement, All exists in perfect harmony. All stand in moment by moment recognition of

Universal unconditional love and through that experience, our dear friend, you will experience physical life as a Soul. This is true human aspect Mastery and a state all will reach, piece by piece, in the right timing.

Compassion is the emotion of Oneness. It is a vibrational quality all have for all have, what some refer to as, the Christ Consciousness within them. It is what makes up the Soul of you. This experience is accessed through alignment. This is what Jesus meant when he said, "No one can enter the kingdom of heaven but through me." This has lost a little bit in the translation for it is meant to mean, "No one can experience heaven on earth without accessing this vibration." He was exampling alignment.

Jesus' messages were all based not only in the Love vibration where they formulated from, but in self-responsibility and self-love for only when one loves themselves are they able, possibility-wise, to love another authentically. This has nothing to do with 'what have you done for me lately?' (We like to show a little levity for we like to see our partner chuckle with us, but we digress...) This has only to do with Soul recognition first in ones Self, then and simultaneously, the probability of experiencing it through others. He exampled this for all and as he exampled and taught Love himself, he too expanded his awareness and ultimately and simultaneously expanded the awareness of the Universe, for when One expands, The All expands. His message is that heaven on earth is found through One's vibration. As the collective vibration raises - expands to include more possibilities - the New Earth will be formed around it. The New Earth is currently a vibrational place that is attainable through alignment with your Soul and it, like all physical manifestations, will be brought forth into physical form through this alignment.

Some of our human friends believe Love is a choice. They are correct in their words however the choice lies in the choosing of alignment. It is not the choosing of a feeling unless that feeling is felt from experiencing the state of alignment. This is

Universal alignment as well for when one is connected to and in alignment with the Soul of them, they are in alignment with the Soul of God as well for it cannot be another way. It is where the Oneness of the Universe is found.

So, in short, every time you feel love, you are feeling your Soul's vibration. Each time you feel perceived pain you believe stems from lost love or rejection and the like, you are feeling the illusory separation from the love of your Soul, and this has nothing to do with what is happening outside of yourself or through the means of another. It is a reaction to the ego's warnings for there is no 'bad' love or no 'lost' love for you cannot lose your Soul nor can it cause you emotional pain for all emotional pain stems from siding with and believing the billboards the ego is placing in front of you. From the Soul's perspective, this is never the case for the Soul knows (and ultimately you as the human aspect is privy to) Who it is and therefore Knows Who You Are as well for you are the Same. You might say your Soul is the seed within the fruit and you, in this analogy, are the meat of the fruit. As you continually choose to be lead by the Soul's perspective, your awareness goes beyond that of any billboard or signage that is set up along your path. This is the action of Love. This is the choosing of your reality.

COLLECTIVE CHOOSING

Every experience you have is first defined vibrationally by you,
and is experienced vibrationally by All.
The collective Soul of God
experiences everything you individually
experience simultaneously.
This is what makes up
the human collective consciousness of the planet.
It is collectively fluid
and is based on the dominant vibration of the Whole.
It is the collective consciousness of the awareness
of the dominant vibration
and is the flow by which the momentum is directed.
If your individual experiences are fear based,
you are simultaneously imploding that vibration
on everyone and everything in the third realm
of consciousness.
You are either contributing to the collective vibration of love or
to that of the vibration of fear. It is your choice
in each moment
as to how you choose to define the experiences you are living.
Your vibrations are the manifestations of the way you think,
which can be redirected in a moment
by a shift in thought perspective.
Love and fear are opposite vibrations, one pure light
and the other pure darkness from where there is
no view and no awareness of Ones' true self.
Choose wisely, my friend.

THE SOUL AND FEAR

As we've suggested in earlier Volumes of this series, the fear factor is presented by the ego aspect in order to in fact, assist the human aspect by offering moment by moment opportunities for choosing (by providing contrast) to allow the human aspect to remain focused on the Soul's perspective while in the physical third dimensional earth plane. That's number one. The contrast, or fear, that is presented is, simply put, for the purpose of giving the human aspect the wherewithal and the indication that it is out of alignment with the Soul's perspective at any given time.

Having said that, the fear that becomes present as the human aspect begins to move in the direction of Love and out of the path of the ego's presentations, is the fear of the unknown. It is the unknown vibration that the ego focuses on and translates into loss of control at the time when the Soul is calling the human aspect forward toward love and toward a more expanded view of itself. This means as you move forward on your path, your eternal path that is, and you continue to expand through faith and through the allowance of the Soul to lead and guide you, the illusion of fear that you experience is in the unfamiliarity of the new vibration that you are stepping into.

As we encourage the allowing of your Soul to lead you, this is encouraging moment by moment living, which is vibrational living, which is the existence in the fifth dimensional plane or the vibrational plane of the New Earth you see. It makes sense that the human who is existing in the third dimensional realm where fear is common place, where the ego aspect is very busy keeping up with all the clutter that surrounds the 'two of you', that it would be very easy to become fearful of a step that is not seen as of yet. We have described this 'walk', this pathway and the creation of this pathway, to our friend Cindy as the 'pre-paving' of your journey. It is the dropping of the paver in front of you almost simultaneous to the stepping upon it. The shift toward the New Earth is one of moment by moment living, trusting and having faith in who you really are which is the extension of your Soul, the God within you.

As we've discussed and as we like to offer as a visual, the Soul could be seen as on the mountain top, hovering over the earth and being aware of and cognizant of all that is happening outside of you. From this 'bird's eye' view, the Soul has all the knowledge it needs to direct you smoothly toward the opportunities that will advance you to the experiences that will help to fulfill its purpose on earth which is always grounded in Love. From this mountain top view, the Soul sees all potholes and sees all road construction, if you will, and will maneuver you around the obstacles, one step at a time, if it is allowed to participate. The Soul, in essence, is leading you, its human aspect, toward and into unchartered vibrational territory. It leads you toward the bigger part of you, the expanded you, where you will ultimately expand your vibrational awareness to walk the earth as a Soul with a physical body Who contains all attributes and powers of the Soul of God. This is life on the New Earth.

So this fear, the fear of the unknown to the human aspect, is an illusion as are all fear based situations. However, the fear is not in the unknown for the Soul. The Soul knows all and knows the route to take you to avoid the pot holes and obstructions along the way, unless they are necessary for the individual expansion of Love. This knowing is within the human aspect as well and the only necessary component is the human aspect's choice to trust. It is the trust in the knowing of who you really are as the Soul, the larger part of you. It is letting go of the control you assume you need in the third dimension and allowing the Soul to give you the impulses to move forward. The way is always made clear when there is faith and trust. When you trust in your Soul, you are trusting in the likes of the One some of you call God.

THE SOUL'S JOURNEY IN THE PHYSICAL WORLD

As we touched on in Volumes One and Two, the Soul journeys to the physical realm in order to expand its awareness and conscious 'level' of love. When this choice is made, as in all choices, it not only effects the individual Soul, but the Collective Soul of God as well. In order to expand in this sense, the human aspect sense that is, the human aspect of the Soul must be subject to contrast. In contrast, there is opportunity for choice. You see, this is the way the human aspect of the Soul expands as well - through choice - and when one aspect of the Soul expands, the Universe expands simultaneously.

The Soul's mission on earth is to expand the love of the Universe through experiences and choices that offer opportunity for expansion. Contrary to popular belief, there are no mistakes, no wrong choices. There are only experiences through which the human aspect is given opportunity to choose. Since, as Abraham says, "you cannot get it wrong and you never get it done," there can be no wrong experience for all experiences result in opportunities to choose, even if the human aspect doesn't recognize it as such. This is due to the vibrational agreement with the ego's offerings and not the Soul.

Some of our human friends will scoff at that understanding and will state situations that, in the human-ego sense, appear to be wrong or bad or detrimental to the life of the human. However, this is never the case for the Soul is on an event-driven timeline where no clocks and no ending exists you see. From the Soul's perspective, the human aspect is in constant motion forward and the time it takes to get from point A to point B does not exist in that realm. There are no barriers and no limits on anything from the Soul's perspective therefore its human aspect can do no 'wrong'. It simply experiences something which creates another opportunity to choose. This is the journey and the process of Soul expansion.

This falls into the category some of our human friends refer to as "wasted time." We hear you say from time to time, "I wasted ten years of my life with that person" or "What a waste of time that was!" For whatever reason is present at the time, whether it is due to a relationship, a job or a choice that didn't go as expected, the situation matters not. There is no such thing as "a waste of time" from the Soul's perspective of its journey because all choices, all experiences are opportunities for more choosing. The Soul understands that it expands in the earth plane through choosing. If one choice is made by the human aspect that is based in fear, another opportunity will come for the sole purpose of choosing again. This choosing comes from the heart and when that shift is made, from the head to the heart, the opportunities to choose love over fear abound.

The Soul experiences the physical world through the experiences of the human aspect. When allowed, the Soul will, through vibrational impulses, guide the human aspect down the path of experiences that will offer more opportunities for choosing love over fear. It is when the human aspect accepts and forms agreements with outside influences, therefore accepting guidance from other places, it strays off course and out of alignment with the Soul's purpose on earth. In this instance, the Soul waits patiently for the human aspect to 'come back around' and seek guidance from its Source once again. This 're-grouping' is done through choosing for when one is out of alignment with the Soul, a choice based in love is what brings it back to wholeness once again.

There is never wasted emotion. There is never wasted time for from the Soul's perspective, all experiences are opportunities for choosing one's way to alignment, regardless of 'how long it takes' for the Soul recognizes change and shift from moment to moment, not year to year or lifetime to lifetime, for the lifetime of the Soul is eternal. The timeframe of the Soul is eternal. A physical life-time for the Soul, the human aspect of the Soul that is, is an experience chosen by the Soul for the purpose of expansion of itself and of the Universe as One. The length of 'time' it is focused in the earth plane is not based on linear time, you see, but experiences. When the Soul has completed its purpose, whether it lasts for a day, a week or one hundred years, it turns its focus elsewhere and the human experience is over. To the Soul, this experience is an event. It is an event chosen because of the opportunities for choice that exist in the earthly plane where there is contrast.

Simply put, each time the Soul visits the earth plane by way of the human aspect, it adds all the experiences it has to its eternal journey and when you leave the earth plane, you as the human aspect of the Soul, the Soul of you has expanded by all the choices in love you made, all the joy you experienced, and all the joy and love you extended to another. It has expanded - you have expanded - because of the experiences you have had. We say to you again, choose your experiences by the opportunities to experience love that are put in your path. These opportunities are offered by your Soul.

THE HEART OF THE SOUL

We were having this conversation with our partner, the conversation about where the heart is located and the question that was posed was, "We are taught by many that the Soul is in the heart. Is that right?"

Our response went something like this: The heart of the human that is referred to by many who teach this way of thought is what we would refer to as the "heart space." This is a conversation about Consciousness, not an organ in your body. The heart is the central point in the body, yes, however the heart 'space' we are referring to is the Soul or the body's Consciousness that is God.

Consciousness is an interesting term that is used by many and misunderstood by many as well. The body lives within the Consciousness, not the other way around for no body or no 'thing' could contain the Consciousness that gives you your aliveness, you see. Without the Consciousness of your Creator, your Source, your Soul, you would not be alive, for the Consciousness is what provides the 'living' part of your being and it is indestructible and eternal.

You see, we are pure Consciousness but we have no body and we are very alive, we promise you that. Nothing that experiences Consciousness dies, for there is no such thing as death. There is only transformation and evolvement. There is no 'going back' to anything for the motion of the Universal Consciousness is forward motion, gaining momentum through the pure Love vibration that is sometimes referred to as the Christ, God Consciousness. Your Soul is that ever-expanding Consciousness.

The Consciousness that is your Soul and your human aspect (and all the aspects of you as well) is your connection to the Oneness of God. It is the heart of God so to speak. This heart, this Consciousness, is also what makes up the Universal Soul for the true purpose of the Soul is to experience Love. Each experience of Love, expands the heart. Yours and everybody's as well.

Our human friends believe the heart of the body is what keeps the human alive. It certainly helps however, the true life of the body is this heart space, this heart consciousness for anybody who is alive in consciousness is alive in the physical realm. And yes, it depends on how you define alive.

We have said over and over, and will continue to say over and over, that there is no death. Death is merely a shift of perspective. It is the Consciousness shifting and expanding as it shifted and expanded prior to its incarnation. This is constant motion and is all directed by the heart of God which is the Soul's Consciousness. This Consciousness moves and expands itself through Love.

THE ORIGIN OF THE SOUL

We begin this section that may seem as if we are describing the origin of your world but we are not, for your Soul is limitless and timeless. It is the mover of momentum through the eternal process. It has no beginning and no end which is a difficult concept for our human friends to understand because of your attachment to linear time. The Soul, again, is timeless.

Your Soul, the God-ness of the you that is experiencing the physical realm of Consciousness, is the aspect of God that is expressing itself in the realm of contrast in order to expand. We have discussed contrast in Volumes One and Two and we will continue to discuss it because it is the very essence, the very manifestation, that creates choice. You are experiencing the contrast as you move forward simply by focusing in the physical realm.

This subject of origin is a human scientific theory. It is a 'must have' in the thoughts and minds of your scientists, your theologians and your teachers of philosophy, however all these theories and concepts and 'fact based' findings are based on what is known - so far.

You see, in your world of time and space, you, the collective 'you', must rely on what has been said or discovered before in order to move ahead. However, this is not how the vibration of the universe works, per se. Your theories and your concepts are in alignment with what you have discovered, based on your theories and concepts of those prior findings - so far. As you move ahead and move into the higher vibrations of light, more possibilities will enlighten your scientists, doctors and theologians and will cause change in the prior findings. Our partner is asking for an analogy and we will offer one here.

The drugs on your planet, those that are developed for purpose of 'curing' disease, are always in the process of discovery. Each and every one - for all drugs, any drug, does not manifest results the same way in all. Now, we will say that some appear to have a healing component, that is true and is based on vibrational agreement, as are all things. However, not all drugs deliver the same reaction in all people. That is evidenced. So as these and more drugs are in the experimental phase, they continue to deliver more and more contrast, more and more uses or non-uses, as it were, to the population who are using them for one thing or another. The longer you use them for more and more people, more is discovered about them whether all are made aware of this or not. This is the natural process of discovery. The same is truth for the origin of your Soul.

Those who have transcended your time space reality in what you call your death process have discovered this once again. Each time you transform into pure positive energy, or 'go home' as some refer to it, you re-emerge into a higher vibration of light. The Soul expands from the human aspect experiences in the earth plane to more possibilities because of the choices it made while experiencing the contrasting world. When this re-emergence takes place, the One-ness is not only felt, but is known as well. In other words, all your theories and concepts of time and space go by the wayside and you experience the Oneness of the Universe once again.

We are not trying to discourage or to argue with the current findings, for we do not argue. We vibrate. The current findings, those that are focused upon and discovered are the discoveries made possible by the expansion of those before you, for your planet has expanded vibrationally by leaps and bounds over the last fifty years of your time. As you have also discovered through this process, the more you discover, the more there is to discover. Yes, because your Universal world is timeless and limitless, you hold yourselves in bondage by your own thinking of the limits you impose on yourselves and your findings. As you move forward and the scientists and theologians discover more and more, they - you - will discover the role these processes play in the path to Oneness for that is your purpose and that is your collective chosen scientific pathway 'home'. It is the pathway for some to the New Earth where the discoveries will simply take you there by presenting the next logical step, one after another. That is one way to do it. There are limitless ways as there are limitless ways to the discovery of and acknowledgment of your own Soul and it's power in the world of contrast. Some of you take one way, some take another and some take yet another and all are correct, for there is no mistake and no timeline for mistakes that exists outside of your current realm of contrast. Limits are imposed on you by you. It's as simple as that. Free yourself from the lower realms of vibration and open your mind to a new way of thinking, one that contains no limits, for outside of yourself, there are none.

All thought about the origins of humanity only causes momentum for discovery and your planet would not be where it is today if not for the curiosity of those who bring their thoughts to pass by their curiosity, focus and determination for new-ness. This is the nature of the human aspect which, through its means to choose thought and to discover the Universe through whatever means is available, naturally contributes to the expansion of not only the individual Soul but the Soul of God as well. This is, again, the Universal Soul - the All - your God.

Thank those who offer the contrast for without it there would be no evolution in which to play. There would be no 'more' to discover and there would be no more Love to be felt for one is as important as the other for without the 'diseased' vibration on your planet, there would be no perceived need for a cure and without perceived need in this case, there would be less evolvement of the Universal vibration of Love.

SOUL TO SOUL LOVE

As we've said, the Soul is 'comprised' of the pure love vibration, this IS what you refer to as Love, in all its versions, if you will. It is the purest vibration that can exist which is why it continues to expand itself to cover more territory so to speak. This is what happens in the expansion of you as the human aspect. When the human aspect expands in love, the Soul and all other aspects expand as well.

When it comes to Soul to Soul love, as we explained in our section about what you refer to as 'falling in love' with another, the human aspect of you is in alignment with your Soul which creates the opportunity for your human aspect to be 'in love' or in alignment with the Whole of You which is the God Soul or the All. When you experience love in this way, you are experiencing the Oneness of God.

Fifth dimensional living or living on the New Earth is the experience of this Oneness. Currently, this is experienced vibrationally in your time-space reality which means it is accessible to the human aspect upon his or her expansion of their own awareness. As we've said before, as you expand your awareness, you include the vibrational patterns and vibrational awareness of more, and that 'more' currently exists in other realities, as do all thought vibrations.

Our partner recently went through a segment of understanding with her dear brother in the understanding of the common thread of the conversation of 'reality' in his world which happens to be real estate. In his world, real estate, this industry of money in exchange for property or housing, is dictated by what one has to spend, therefore turning over the power of the 'market' and allowing an illusion to dictate the power of the Soul's desire. This, in the third dimension, is logical and time sensitive as these markets in your world fluctuate due to many factors, none of which are said to be controlled by the human in the sense that they are believed to be linked to and unchangeable by the human, only by the 'market' and what the 'market bears' at any given time.

This line of thinking is, from a multi-dimensional standpoint, old paradigm in that this 'market' that is said to drive the industry cannot exist without the human consciousness which makes up all markets and drives all of your industry. However, in this case, the argument he makes, stating, 'you can see reality clearly' is the standard response to anyone stating her case that vibration runs everything. This is an example of the limitations he has imposed on himself as do millions like him, driven and influenced by what is 'seen' as reality. This demonstrates a misunderstanding of the term 'reality' and how reality is expressed, and is a common understanding amongst our human friends and is the cause for self-imposed limitations. "What you see is what you get" is a common theme as well which helps to enforce the old adage, if you can't see it, it doesn't exist. However, as the collective human consciousness expands naturally, the limitations will begin to dissolve as more and more proof for the human mind is eventually exposed.

To understand the multi-dimensional reality, one must understand the power of the Soul's natural ability to expand itself into the other realities that exist by way of thought vibration; by way of the pure love vibration where all possibilities exist. The is the space where all creation begins. The more expansive one becomes, the more possibilities exist therefore creating the space for other realities to reveal themselves in the physical plane. Unless and until these realities are understood, other realities are 'out of touch' to those who resist their own expansion. Your beloved scientist, Albert Einstein, was not the only one prior to now to explain it this way, "Everything is energy and that is all there is to it. Match the frequency to the reality you want and you cannot help but get that reality. It cannot be any other way. This is not philosophy. This is physics."

Our partner is wondering what this example has to do with Soul to Soul Love and we say this: Soul to Soul love is the expansive nature of the human ability to see the Soul in another; to see themselves in another, in all others in fact. It is the seeing - the experiencing past the third dimensional self and third dimensional reality into the expansive nature of the human aspect of the Soul. This is true love indeed. But we digress.

The example that was given in the earlier paragraph about the misunderstanding of the multi-dimensional self and its power to dictate its own reality is a common thread among the third dimensional human aspect as most 'sit' today. The human aspect who believes it is limited to its human self, limits its own expansion beginning with its beliefs about its own abilities. Further along in the discussion, the brother said, "we are all limited in our lives" and then made a comparison to money because of the discussion that was happening at that time about the housing market. This core belief, this belief that most carry about their own limitations, spans many areas of the physical experience if it is allowed to pave the way so to speak. Our friends Abraham teach, "a belief is just a thought you keep on thinking" which opens many doors for opportunity to change and to shift your thought processes, first about your own abilities which fosters the belief in others' abilities as well. This is a step in the understanding of who you really are which is creator; you are creators first and foremost and the creation begins with your thoughts and the beliefs you have about yourselves and your ability to create your own reality.

As we bring this back around to Soul to Soul Love and the expansive nature of the human aspect of the Soul, we invite you to consider the following scenario for a moment.

Let us look at these two human aspects we have been exampling for you. Let us look at our partner's perspective of reality first which is an expanded version of the ability to create a reality of love, peace and joy on a level that is always expanding. This level, she expects to experience, continues to expand as she allows her awareness of more to unfold as she sets her desires in the fore-front of her mind and continues to focus upon them, as the opportunities for manifestation reveal themselves. Soon she is holding the reins by way of her focused thoughts, and allowing her all-knowing Soul to lead her in the direction of her desire for more. As she continues to allow this unfolding by allowing the participation of her Soul, she experiences more of her multi-dimensional being and its abilities to expand, exampled in Volume 2 of this series. This is true alignment. This is the seamless relationship between the Soul and the human aspect and an example of the Oneness that is the way to the creation of the New Earth in the physical plane.

Now we will look at the beliefs, influenced by the third dimensional society, which result in the version of reality her brother is currently living, as most are. As the earth plane continues to expand its own consciousness, as we've said before, this opens up opportunities for the human collective to expand with it meaning expand individually and (simultaneously) collectively to form this New Earth. Each individual is being exposed to opportunities that are manifest because of the new level of awareness that is now being offered, however each individual, their free will and choice intact, will choose whether to expand or not. This expansion comes from the desire and willingness to explore their own beliefs and thought processes and to open up to experiencing a new way of life which brings with it new manifestations and therefore, physical change.

Her dear brother then has the belief we discussed which is controlled and seemingly 'hardened' by what society dictates; where all potential buyers of this specific group are held and in essence, all respond to this 'market' the same way. This is what we call 'collective grouping' which means all who belong to this particular group - this market bearing group - have the same beliefs about how their reality will play out. They believe their reality, their "this is what is" life, is a product of the outside sources and influences of society, money and whatever the market will bear at any given time, that nothing can change the way things are if not driven by the workings of this 'market'.

This is one example of the self-imposed limitations of collective grouping and as you ponder this term, you will begin to see other versions all around you. It is rampant in your religious sects, your political arena, your food industry, your medical society, your entertainment world, etc., etc. Simply put, most people believe more of what they read, what they hear and what others tell them is true than they do of their own Soul's knowing. Herein lies the core issue with the situations you are now faced with on your planet. Who is right and who is wrong? The self-constructed battle continues and will continue until the recognition of who you really are, individually and collectively, is acknowledged freely, and that is that you are multi-dimensional beings, multi-faceted with the ability to experience the Soul of you, the God-ness of you if you prefer, in the physical plane with a shift in your perspective of your own beliefs. It matters not what the others are doing although the argument is made moment by moment that that is the only thing that matters and if you continue to compare the individual nature of the human aspect with the individual nature of another, you will continue to form your collective groups and live in the third dimensional plane of contrast.

The belief that you are all the same in the third dimensional realm is only truth when viewed from the Soul's perspective of pure love in the recognition of the Oneness and when that happens, Soul to Soul Love will manifest in the creation of the New Earth on the physical plane. This creation is one of Love and is currently in the vibrational realm, available and ready to be experienced by you, at your vibrational request.

Soul to Soul Love is the mixture that will ultimately manifest the New Earth in the physical realm. This event is timing based and will unfold as the events before it manifest to bring it forth, mainly the event of each individual's acknowledgement of the multi-dimensional nature of the Self, the human aspect Self of the Soul.

DELIBERATE EXPANSION

Many of our human friends, including our partner who's typing these words, ask us, "how does one get into alignment?" Cindy has asked us many, "but how do I..." questions which of course we're happy to answer however she's asking (and perhaps you are as well) 'how' and we say 'you feel it.'

Expansion isn't something you 'do' with action. Expansion is the manifestation of increased awareness. This comes through focus. Now we're not saying you can't 'do' things, physical things, to assist in your expansion, in fact we're giving you a process to assist here. It is a vibrational process that is felt, not thought.

Each time anyone, for any reason, expands in Love, the All expands with them. Everything expands naturally. For example, each time you express love for someone or something, you are expanding. This is not deliberate in most cases, but by default if you will. It is not necessary to 'do' anything to expand as it is the natural state and purpose of your eternal Soul. You just focus on the feeling of the manifestation. You create this manifestation through your vibrational feeling. You focus on imagining the feeling of it.

Love manifests itself in many ways, one of which is expansion. When you are in alignment with your Soul, you are feeling what the Soul is. In other words, you are free of resistance. This is how your Soul feels. When you are free of resistance, you are in the expanding mode, so to speak, and as you expand your awareness, you are allowing more opportunities for more expansion which means more opportunities to love, to feel love, to be love, are present.

So, we'd like to offer you an easy process to expand your awareness. We tested it out on our partner and it has become an alternative way for her to feel love, to feel her true being. This is really all we're after and that is to get you to 'feel' more and 'think' less. We're not a huge fan of processes as such because we know that all are very different and not all processes work for everyone as we exampled in Volume Two. However, this process is fluid meaning it can be interpreted any way you like and it will still work.

We will describe the process first and how we walked Cindy through it and then we'll comment.

Step 1:

Relax and breathe. Fill your lungs and slowly release. This will help in the relaxing. We would repeat this a few times. Whatever is comfortable. (Our partner was in a meditative state when we introduced this to her. She was wearing headphones, listening to peaceful music and intended to simply relax her mind. For some of you, this could be through painting or drawing, some through gardening or reading. Anyplace you go to quiet yourself will be fine. It is your choice.) Our partner describes this Step (now that she knows what's coming) as "preparing the canvas."

Step 2:

Imagination. We'd like for you, in this relaxed state, imagine if you will a peaceful, joyful scene that excites your passion. It may be some place you've been or someplace you've never been but desire to visit. It could be walking down a beautiful street in the rain or driving through the mountains in the fall. The intention here is to create in your mind, a pathway that surrounds you with joy. Our partner, a lover of Central Park in New York, chose the pathway underneath the Cherry Blossom trees. She created it the way she wants to experience it meaning she added beautiful flat cobblestones as her walkway, and as she strolled under the trees, she smelled the cherry blossoms in full bloom. She added the perfect temperature and dressed herself in beautiful clothing that added to the picture-perfect scene. As she looked to the left, she saw a beautiful beach and when she looked to the right, she experienced a beautiful chateau high in the mountains. The intention here is to create the personal and individual pathway to your Soul by surrounding yourself with those visuals that bring you joy to think about. These thoughts will manifest into the love vibration, the natural state of the Soul and voila! You will be in alignment. This is vibrational agreement at its best.

Step 3.

As you stroll, you create what is in front of you, moment by moment. It's as if with each step you take, a new picture appears and it is the timeline you are currently walking, side by side with your Soul. The human aspect releases the ego aspect, vibrationally, and walks the earth as a Master and at One with God.

As you are strolling this pathway, it becomes more and more peaceful and lighter. You visualize up ahead the bright light - the manifested vibration of your Soul. This is where you are expanding to include, you see. This is a journey 'out' or as some would say 'up'; It is the process of the expansion of your vibrational awareness and you are expanding to the place and 'vicinity' of your Soul. This is what alignment is. This is, in essence, putting yourself into alignment by way of this pathway you are creating. Line it with anything and everything that brings you complete joy whether it (or he/she) exists in this physical realm or not. It - whatever 'it' is - exists in its vibrational state - always. This is truth whether the human acknowledges it or not. And this vibration is the key to expansion. But we digress....

As you continue the momentum in the direction of expansion of love, your vibration expands as well and soon, moment by moment, the path ahead of you is clear and the proverbial "light at the end of the tunnel" view is bright white. It is the pure vibration of your Soul surrounding you more and more as you gravitate to closer proximity. In other words, as you move out of the denseness.

Step 4.

As you are visualizing and creating this pathway, you are vibrationally walking it. This is the creative process. It is the creating of the visual of your individual pathway, with the 'Soul' purpose of experiencing it. As you continue to move forward, you are moving in the direction of your Soul evidenced by the lightness you continue to move through. Your physical body will experience this 'lightening' by way of vibration; some will feel an intensity build as they move closer to the vicinity of their Soul's vibration. (To our partner...Said this way, it implies the Soul's vibration is not within the human aspect's vibration and this, of course, is not the case. It happens this way.... the Soul's vibration is always the underlying vibration of the human aspect, less the amount of fear based vibration you allow in, so to speak. 'In' your awareness that is.) So, as you are moving forward, you are naturally releasing the lower vibrations that are holding you within those vibratory fields. This movement and releasing allows more of your underlying vibration, that of the Soul, to emerge and your experience is that of a new vibrational timeline; it is the eternal timeline of the Soul.

Cindy added and experienced floral smells and music as well because these things bring her joyful peace and they allow her to have this experience in many different ways by changing it and causing it to evolve through love by adding other love vibrations to the mix. It is in effect, what you might call an experiential vision board.

Step 5.

In Cindy's experience, she had brief encounters with others in her Soul family who exist on many different vibrational timelines. You may 'run into them' as you cross paths, so to speak. While in this realm remember, more is possible. Once you're outside the fearful vibration, your opportunity to experience love is much wider so to speak. As you've experienced, other aspects of you who have played a role in this incarnation with and for you, the collective You that is, will re-emerge as well for they have their homes too. So yes, this is one way to move through other dimensions; it is the choosing of the vibrational path done consciously, not by default. It is the true creation process - the creation of your reality at any level you choose and it is simultaneously the creation of and evolution of the Universe itself.

As our friends Abraham say, "One in Alignment is more powerful than a million who are not." This is the space you want to create from. It is the vibration of abundance and pure loving energy. Anything and everything created from this space will thrive as it is meant to exist, in whatever form and forever long. All creations from this space are eternal. This is the reality and the viewed focus of the Universal Soul that is God.

This vibrational space is what Abraham refers to as The Vortex. It is the point of creation for the Universe and it holds within it the realm of all possibilities. It is the space Jesus refers to in the quote, "All things are possible for those who believe." If you believe other realms of consciousness exist, you have the power within you to experience them.

Quotes & Commentary
By Josef...

You See,
The Light Is
The Manifestation
Of The Vibration
That Heals
And Where
There Is Light,
There Is
No Darkness.

In a nutshell,

This universe is choice-based. The vibration is a match to whatever choice of thought you make. This thought choice, if focused upon enough (your deliberate choosing of thought) is your future manifestation. The manifestation occurs when the vibration of the thought and the vibration of the universe come together and vibrate in agreement with each other. This is your creative process whether you do it deliberately or by default.

Your physical reality presents itself as manifestations of your thoughts; your thoughts about how to live your life, through your beliefs about the world and your place within it, through your thoughts about yourself and Who You Really Are, and through the limitations you put on your own being. It is a perfect manifestation of your vibrational agreement with all those things, beginning with the thoughts you believe about yourself.

If you can, perceive the 'what is' that you are currently experiencing in vibrational terms. Then, perceive it differently, as the artwork you are creating. Perceive it as 'old news' as Abraham calls it, in that it is the manifestation of previous thoughts and focus.

To create a new reality of one thing or your physical experience, all that is necessary is a shift in your perception and your perspective of how creation works. It creates through choice and that choice is directed by you whether you acknowledge it or not, whether you use the universal laws to your benefit or not. The law is consistent and is something you can rely on to be evident to you if you choose to include it in your awareness. This is the creation of expanded awareness. Look what you've done! Rejoice and continue to create each step of the way. Choose the thought and the experience and watch the universe deliver it to you. Choose alignment.

The Experience Of Love Is The Physical Manifestation Of The Vibration Of The Soul.

In a nutshell,

All vibration manifests itself in some way either by way of emotion, physical change, changes to your physical reality and the like. You are living your manifestations. In other words, your life is a series of manifestations brought forth through your focused thought vibrations. This how your life experience comes into being.

When you are in alignment with your Soul, meaning allowing the aspect of you 'Who knows more' to direct your path, you have guidance from a higher perspective, a perspective that is centered in Love. As you focus and intend to allow your Soul to lead, your experiences are then created by the Soul's vibration of Love, offering the opportunity for manifesting, for its human aspect, a physical experience of the loving purpose it desires.

There is opportunity for choosing love in each moment and each time anyone does, or any collectively do, the beneficiary of that choice is the Universe, beginning with yourself and expanding out from there to include the All. Yes, Love is a big deal.

Because Love is a Soul vibration, it is not judged by its duration because there isn't one. Love never ceases. Love is eternal and expands through experiences of it, as well. Through you, in fact. It matters not if Love 'lasts' for one moment or a lifetime, its value is the same. Love is a steady, ever increasing bolt of vibration that is always available. You have the opportunity to choose it in every moment, by choosing alignment with your Soul or not. You may choose not to choose it for a day, a week, a month or a year. However consistently you choose the other, those choices never weaken the strength or the existence of the stream of Love. When you are ready to choose again, it is available. This too, is the nature of your Soul.

When You Feel Authentic Love, You Are Experiencing Your Own Expansion. It Is Spontaneous (And Simultaneous) Combustion.

In a nutshell,

The word Love has been given many, many meanings, some of which do it justice and some that don't. If there is any fear present when Love is brought into the situation, it is a false description. For example, if one is beating on another and the reason for staying is referred to as Love, this is misguided information.

Having said that, true Love, being 'in' authentic love, is the recognition from Soul to Soul. It is what some have referred to as 'Soul mates' of which there are many for each of you. They come in many different forms and are recognized by the Oneness.

Our partner was present when 'love at first sight' was experienced by her friend. This event happened many many years ago however she still can recount the experience of witness, moment by moment as when a divine connection appears and is visible to our human friends, it is a remembering of Who They Are, evidenced by what they're watching. It is the observer and the participator simultaneously recognizing the presence of the Soul of another. It's a beautiful thing indeed.

The Soul connection is one that is mostly indescribable by our human friends because it is a vibrational connection and it is tough to describe a vibration unless one has experienced it in some form or another. The Love that you are, the Soul that you Are, is that love vibration and when One 'finds' another in this sense, whether it be a relationship love, a kinship love, or a friendship love, they are all the same vibration. The sameness, once again, is in the recognition of the Soul's vibration.

As we discussed in the prior Volumes, there are many aspects of your Soul and all aspects have other aspects as well, simply put. You have what has been referred to by our partner as 'Soul families' where those who have 'signed on' to travel to the physical realm together to assist each other at the appointed time, come back together or yes, find each other by way of vibration. This is the simultaneous combustion! For it is a vibrational agreement in the making from eons ago. You may have experienced something like this and you couldn't quite make out what was happening or what was drawing you to this particular person. This is a vibrational meeting that was planned prior to your incarnation and when the coming together event happens, there is celebration on many levels for you have both met your spiritual agreement to assist in this next phase of your journey in a sense, for there are no happenstance meetings of the Souls. Each meeting is pre-planned, event driven, and the recognizable portion of the human aspect in these meetings, is through the Soul. It is the Soul's vibration calling Its matching vibration to itself and it is always the perfect match for that moment in timing.

The expansion occurs when the Soul of another is recognized. When one can experience this type of connection, it allows others like it to follow suit, allowing the 'seeing' of Souls in others. Now, we are not saying that you must be 'in love' with everyone you see although you are from your Soul's perspective. But from the human aspect's perspective, to utilize your ability to see beyond their focus upon the ego's warning signs, and see them for Who They Really Are, is the expansion of your own vibration. When this happens, when you allow this to happen, you are expanding not only your own vibration but simultaneously expanding the possibilities surrounding you.

We believe the path of least resistance to this point is through the relationship love for it is the way most of our human friends have allowed themselves to feel. Once this connection is 'felt', it is then recognizable in other ways. However, once this vibration is experienced, it is sought after vibrationally. It's as if you are tasting chocolate for the first time. Knowing there is more to be had, you search it out only in this case, your searching is vibrational.

If Your Ego
Wasn't Doing Its Job,
You Would
Never Know
When You're
Out of Alignment
With Your Soul.
Alignment
With Your Soul
Is The Path
To All Abundance.

In a nutshell,

Our partner has been saying for some time now, "The ego gets a bad rap" and we agree which is part of the purpose of this healing series. As you seek and find relief of any kind, it offers opportunity for vibrational expansion toward Love.

There have been teachings and many forms of interpretation of the ego and its role for many years, most of which have been, from our perspective, misleading. The teaching that the ego is 'evil' or that one must 'do without the ego' is a teaching based in fear which naturally creates and manifests resistance. In order to create anything, either by way of a teaching or by strong influence and the like - from an outside source - you naturally create momentum. Depending on your vibration and intention, your momentum either flows in the direction of love or fear. If you choose agreement with the signage and warnings of the ego, your physical reality will manifest negative emotion and ultimately, fear based experiences.

Once negative emotion is felt, it is the first clear indication that the ego is doing its job through the path of least resistance. This is the first opportunity the ego is presenting to you for the sole purpose of offering you choice. In other words, the more you think of something that generates negative emotion, the more negative emotion you generate. We like your saying, "making a mountain out of a molehill". It explains the way momentum works in one visual.

The ego is your supplier of the signage - the influence - and you are the supplier of the vibration which is where your choice lies, moment by moment. You are in control of the momentum because you're in control of the vibration, which is dependent on your choice in each moment. In fact, in each moment you are, what you might call, standing at a crossroads and a decision, a choice is before you, equally as powerful in the way of experience. Each has a purpose and they're both to show you the vibrational way to the Soul.

By choosing love in each moment, trust in the Soul's guidance, you are generating an expansion of the love vibration and all benefit. On the flip side of that, by choosing to lament over or precast a situation from your past or not wanted in your future, you are living in the fear vibration and missing each moment of conscious choosing. You have chosen to ignore your own power of creation, so you are creating your reality by default.

For example, most of the NEWS that is broadcast in your world is, let us say from our perspective of course, bad news. If we were naming it, we would don it "OLD BAD NEWS" from the majority of our human friends' perspective, and we would dismiss it. Half of it is old news, manifestation ally speaking, and the other half is speculation. Each half causes the collective momentum to gain speed, if you will, in the direction of fear and as a result, those who 'swim' in it, drown in it too. In other words, in the words of our partner, you choose to go down with the ship.

If you've read the first two Volumes of this work, you understand the perspective of the Soul when it comes to its aspect, the ego, and its role within the human experience. No aspect of the Soul can be, by pure vibrational definition, anything but love based, as it is where the ego is concerned.

The ego is an aspect of the Soul with a purpose which is, perhaps, as a way shower in the third dimensional earth plane for the human aspect. Its purpose, in service to the Soul and its human aspect, is one of an 'indicator' of sorts, who reveals to the human aspect by way of negative emotion, where it is in any given moment in relationship to its state of alignment with their aspect, the Soul. In other words, and in simpler form, the ego points out the contrast of the third dimension to the human aspect through the offering of negative emotion.

This contrasting emotion offers choice to the human aspect. It offers darkness as its choice. It is an indication to the human aspect that its thought of the moment is not in alignment with the thought of its Soul in that same moment. All negative emotion is based in this scenario and never has anything to do with outside circumstance other than it being a catalyst as well. It is an indication of the distance between the vibration of the human aspect and the vibration of the Soul. It is in this 'gap' that negative emotion manifests in its physical form and you feel it. Anytime you feel something, it is the recognition of your vibrational aspects. The negative emotion is a wave from your ego and the love, peace and joy is a high-five from your Soul.

Whatever your situation, whether wanted or unwanted, was created by you and is changeable by you as well. The key is to shift the perspective. It can always improve for there is no ceiling. A desire for more Love, creates a space for more Love and that space is limitless and boundless. Well, yes, it just plain makes for a more enjoyable physical experience which is the point of it all. To Love.

How To
Control Your Emotions:
As Your Soul Guides,
You Feel Love
And All That Goes With It.
As Your Ego Guides,
You Feel Fear
And All That Goes With It.
You Get To
Choose The Experience.
Choose Love.
Just Keep Choosing It.

In a nutshell,

You are at a crossroad of choice in each moment. You either choose your thoughts consciously, knowingly participating in the creation of your reality or, you allow your experience to 'happen' to you based on the collective vibration you stand in agreement with. We will explain.

This statement presents the choosing of either controlled momentum offered up by you, or band-wagon momentum meaning the momentum that flows around you, based on the collective group's vibration at any given time. Collective grouping in this scenario would be exampled by your political parties, a small group of scientists, a group of surgeons perhaps, all dependent on the findings of their group or other groups before them and based on percentages and what they deem as 'proven fact', all based on what is vibrationally available at the time by way of human participation. This is the process of scientific evolution, which is based on human evolution. Everything evolves through choosing.

New Earth living is living by way of your Soul, choosing alignment with the thoughts and vibration of the Soul in each moment for in each moment, there is always choice and this choosing is what creates your reality and contributes to the collective conscious choosing of humanity. The New Earth is a vibrational timeline where no denseness exists. It is the evolved vibration of the earth plane, available to create from and as more choose love, more opportunity for love exists and expansion is experienced. As this vibration is focused upon and the momentum builds in its direction, more and more New Earth vibrational reality is revealed for it is held in this vibration. And you choose to experience it or not.

"They Cannot Say, 'Here It Is Or There It is.' You See, The Kingdom Of God Is Within You."

-Luke 17:21

In a nutshell,

Choosing beliefs about the current available teachings is based on interpretation; the teachings' interpretations of the authors, the scribes, and the channels. Their experiences bring all interpretation to you for yours. The purpose of this is to bring expanded Truth to your awareness. It presents itself to you for your own interpretation based on how it makes you feel. It comes in all forms, through unlimited channels. It comes by way of your own experience, through nature and through the collective consciousness of others.

The most powerful and productive interpretation though, comes through you; it comes through by way of your emotions and your feelings. These are indications of your aspects vying for your attention. It impacts you from within, for the Soul vibration you hold within you is the vibration of God and is the vibration of all knowing. It reveals itself to you in each moment and offers this choosing. It is the choosing of the human aspect and is subject to all that surrounds it. Know this: Moment by moment choosing from within is the choosing of the Soul and is the example and manifestation of alignment. It is New Earth existence.

I Am
The Stable Part Of You.
I Am The Rock.
I Am
One Rock Off The
Mountain And I Am
The Mountain.
I Am Your View.
You Can See All Of Me
If You Choose.
I Look Through Your Eyes.
I Am You.

In a nutshell,

This is the Oneness of God.

Made in the USA
Las Vegas, NV
13 August 2023

76062042R00039